PILLAR BOX RED

ISBN 978-1-914536-91-5

WELCOME

Trends in video games come and go, but there's been one titan that has truly proven itself to be the undeniable mainstay: Minecraft.

Who would've ever thought that in an industry filled with next-gen graphics, storytelling and mechanics, a sandbox game made from literal blocks would take the crown? Well, the game's presentation is kind of deceptive in its simplicity - it may look basic, but Minecraft can offer the player a boundless gameplay experience that no other game can.

When it comes to Minecraft, there is no one definitive gameplay experience as there often is with other games. There aren't even like... a vague ten or so - it's literally impossible to quantify. So it would be impossible for one guide to cover the game in its entirety - there's probably even secrets spawning out there that even the most seasoned of Minecraft vets haven't discovered yet.

What the guide does is help you grow your fundamental knowledge of the game and its core mechanics. You can't stumble across a hidden jungle temple and discover its hidden treasure if you can't get past your first day and night cycle. This game is all about exploration, so this guide is here to help build up your foundations to enable you to explore until your heart's content. So let's dive in!

CONTENTS

GLOSSARY

Minecraft may be made up of pixelated blocks, but the world itself is far more complex. There's a whole lexicon of in-game terms and systems that can still make even the most hardened Minecraft miners trip, let alone someone picking up the game for the first time.

That's where this chapter comes in - get ready to boost your mine-specific vocab to max out both your general gameplay and the value of what we'll be chatting about in the next sixty or so pages.

ADVENTURE

Adventure mode is a Minecraft mode that limits the tools available for specific tasks.

ALEX

As the First Lady of Minecraft, Alex is the name of the default female skin for the player character.

AFK

Shorthand for 'away from keyboard'.

BEDROCK

The literal foundation of the Minecraft world. If you're digging down deep and hit bedrock, then that's as far as you're getting.

BIOME

Minecraft's world is simple yet vast, and made up of different ecological regions that we call Biomes. You'd be surprised how versatile blocks can be: from swamps to deserts, jungles to tundras - and each biome has its own unique features and climate. For more information, check out the chapter The World of Minecraft: Biomes on p. 18-21.

BLOCKS

Blocks are the basic units of structure in Minecraft - they come in a wide variety, from cherry blossom and diamonds to lava and suspicious gravel. The majority of blocks can be broken down into some form of resource (like gravel to flint), but some (like the dragon egg) are rarer and can drop an item, or totally indestructible (like bedrock and locked chests).

BLOCK CLUTCH

This move is when you quickly place a block beneath you to break your fall and prevent fall damage. It's a tough move to master, but can save you some hearts if you manage to finesse it.

CHUNK

A measurement used to render distance in Minecraft (16x16 from the sky to bedrock).

COORDS

Short for coordinates, coords note your current position in the Minecraft world, or the position of key items/places you might want to return to.

CRAFT

Crafting is a key Minecraft skill that allows you to create items using resources scavenged from the world around you. Check out more information on the process on p. 36.

CREATIVE

Creative is one of the available game modes. As the name suggests, it eliminates a lot of the survival elements and is more about letting a player exercise their creative side - players have an endless supply of blocks to play around with.

CREEPER

This iconic pile of pixels is an aggressive mob that creeps up (hence the name) on players before exploding. Legend says its victims can still hear its warning hiss even in the afterlife... Learn how to avoid this fate by reading more about Creepers in Mobs of Minecraft (p. 42-45).

CRIT

Short for critical hit, which is when a hit does x1.5 damage instead of the usual x1. Crits can be triggered by jumping and striking your target on the way down. You'll know when you land one because successful Crits are signalled by a brown X on your target.

DROP

When a mob is defeated or a block is destroyed, it usually leaves something behind: this is a drop. Mobs have several possible drops that vary in rarity (Common to Rare) and however you kill them.

THE END

The End is a dark and dangerous dimension, made up of islands dotted around a space-like void and inhabited by some seriously hostile mobs. This shadowy realm is not for the faint-hearted, nor a quick day trip; players usually spend most of the game in the Overworld and Nether training to reach the End and take on its challenges.

ELYTRA

The fabled elytra is a glider - the only method of flight in Survival mode.

ENCHANT

Enchanting is a Minecraft system that really comes to play in later-game survival. It lets you upgrade your gear.

ENDERMAN

This rare mob is a silhouette creature with long limbs.

ENDER DRAGON

The final boss of Minecraft - the Ender Dragon is a huge flying hostile mob that resides in the End. She (yes, it's a girl) is the largest spawning mob in the whole game.

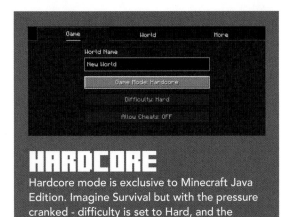

HARDCORE

Hardcore mode is exclusive to Minecraft Java Edition. Imagine Survival but with the pressure cranked - difficulty is set to Hard, and the whole world is deleted if a player dies.

HOTBAR

The first nine slots of your inventory, like a quick access to items you'll probably need on the go.

INVIS

A common shorthand for the invisibility potion.

MOB

The world of Minecraft is teaming with creatures both friendly and hostile, and you'll need to learn which is which if you want a chance of best-utilising their resources and surviving as long as you can. Be sure to check out Mobs of Minecraft on p. 42-45 for more information.

MOD

A mod (short for modification) is anything that changes the base content of the game. Minecraft mods are created by the player base, and can be downloaded and installed into the game to customise the gameplay experience. Not all mods are created equal, however, and it's advised that you be careful which you choose to install; some aren't game-friendly, and could cause issues in how the game runs.

MOJANG

The masterminds and developers of Minecraft.

OVERWORLD

This the default Minecraft world, made up of different biomes and teaming with tons of different Mobs. While it does hold its own challenges (especially thanks to recent updates like Trails & Tales, The Wild and Caves & Cliffs), it's generally seen as a friendly, standard realm compared to the Nether and the End.

PICKAXE

Your old and faithful, the pickaxe will always be your most useful piece of equipment and be there to mine blocks for resources.

PORTAL

If you want to dabble in a touch of interdimensional travel, then you're going to need a portal. Building portals will enable you to hop between the three realms: the Overworld, the End and the Nether.

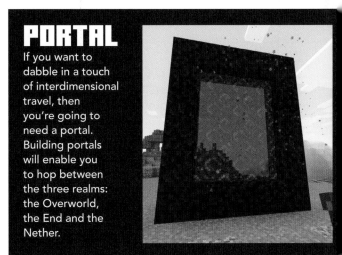

NETHER

The Nether is an alternate dimension and a great deal more treacherous to traverse than the Overworld. We're talking lava, flames and a lot of realm-specific mobs who consider you a delicacy. So yes, it's a tough sell for the Minecraft Tourism Board, but finding a portal to the Nether does mean you'll have access to rare materials and resources… if you survive the trip.

STACK

A stack is a bunch of items together in your inventory in groups of 16 or 64.

STEVE

The main man of Minecraft, Steve is the severely pixelated face of the whole game, and the default male skin for the player character.

SPAWN

A spawn point is where the player starts a game, or returns after they die. Spawn points can be changed by using respawn anchors, or commands like /setworldspawn or /spawnpoint.

SPECTATOR

Truly the chillest of game modes, Spectator allows players to sail through worlds and, well, spectate. Sure, they can't interact with any of the blocks or mobs, but they also don't have to worry about any of the survival elements either.

SURVIVAL

The core Minecraft experience - Survival mode tasks players with gathering materials and resources, crafting tools and items, dodging threats and doing their utmost to survive as long as possible.

VANILLA

This term is used to describe Minecraft in its unaltered form, without any plugins or mods.

XP

Short for experience (also known as EXP), and like life, the game is chock full of it. You can earn XP from practically all of the gameplay mechanics on offer - from social tasks like trading, survival tasks like fishing and bloodthirsty tasks like mowing down some mobs. Mining, breeding, enchanting, using furnaces… you get the picture. Do something = get XP. What's unique about Minecraft's XP is that the experience doesn't change the player's stats or power levels; instead, it can be used to enhance equipment.

PROT

Short for protection, players use this to describe armour enchantments.

PVP AND PVE

These acronyms stand for Player vs Player and Player vs. Environment, respectively.

SANDBOX

This term is used to describe a game with an open world design that allows players the freedom to design, modify and explore the world they're dropped in. A lot of games follow a linear storyline and narrative, but the appeal of sandbox games (like Minecraft) is that it lets the player become a creator, too.

SERVER

An online space where players hang out and play in multiplayer games.

SKIN

While Steve and Alex are iconic and forever, there's also other options to dress your player character. Skins are special costumes that you can use to customise your in-game avatar.

SURVIVAL 101

So what's the name of the game? Besides from Minecraft, obviously? When it comes to gameplay, there's no one definitive way to play - in fact, there are five specific modes: Creative, Adventure, Spectator, Hardcore and the main vibe, Survival.

Players are tasked with gathering resources, fighting mobs when night falls and exploring whatever world that particular game has spawned them into. Whether you want to try it with friends, integrate with NPC villagers or do the whole thing alone - travel to the ends of the Overworld (and beyond) or build your dream home and settle down with some chickens, the aim is to keep doing whatever you want to do for as long as you can.

Survival is Minecraft's core game mode - essentially the other game modes are all riffs on survival, like survival under a certain context (Adventure), survival turned up to 100 (Hardcore), optional survival with all the game's spoils at your fingertips (Creative) and watching someone attempt to survive all of that (Spectator).

 New Recipes Unlocked! Check your recipe book

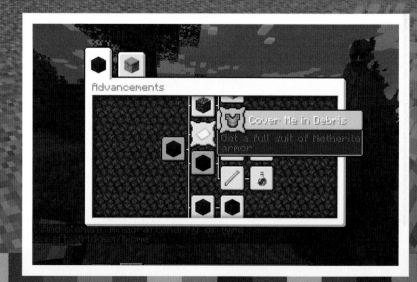

HUNGER AND HEALTH

The basic metrics of survival come down to your Health and Hunger bars. These indicate how close (or far) you are to making it another day in whatever scenario you've decided to play out. You'll find that these bars generally dip down during the day depending on whatever action you're doing (or forced into, if you find yourself ambushed), but you can always recharge by taking a nap in your bed or fixing yourself up a quick snack.

SURVIVING ⇒ THRIVING

Once you get the hang of keeping yourself alive comfortably, then it's time to elevate the situation and upgrade your quality of life a bit. There are four big gameplay mechanics open to you: Crafting, Smelting, Brewing and Enchanting. Crafting will be important from early to late game, but you'll find processes like Brewing and Enchanting really only worth playing with mid-late gameplay.

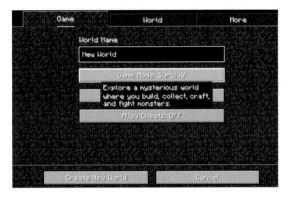

SURVIVAL CHALLENGES

But everyday is a survival challenge, you say. I get it, but the game also offers some real gameplay challenges a bit more taxing than a baby zombie riding the back of a chicken.

Taking on the Ender Dragon: The ender dragon is Minecraft's big bad, icon, legend and final boss. Taking her on means grinding away to acquire the strongest equipment and gear in game, and some of the highest tier potions and enchantments. And that's just to stand a chance. You'll have to master the game's core mechanics in order to prepare for this fight - even finding your way to the End is a Herculean task in itself. If you succeed in your endeavour, you'll win a Dragon Egg to proudly display in your home (or inventory, if it doesn't match the aesthetic you're going for) as a trophy.

Earning Achievements/Advancements: Minecraft also comes with a set of gameplay Achievements (Bedrock Edition) or Advancements (Java Edition). The range of difficulty is as vast as the game itself, rewarding you for opening your inventory to taming every single cat variant or taking on the ender dragon twice. It's quite the checklist to make your way through.

Check out the Michelin Minecraft chapter on p. 16-17 for more information on food and cooking.

RESOURCE REVIEW

The basic unit of structure in the Minecraft world is the block: the perfect resource for you to use in your never ending quest for survival. Whether it's building your first shack or a realm-hopping portal to take on the game's final boss, the world is ready to provide you with whatever you need to do so.

There are over 150 different types of blocks in Minecraft, so here's a quick list of some of the most useful blocks you'll come across.

NATURAL BLOCKS

These blocks can be found in the Overworld and the Nether. As the name suggests, they can be found from nature, and can be harvested and crafted into another resource.

For more information on the Nether realm, check out The Three Dimensions on p. 22.

GROUND

Block	Use
Dirt	A good block for farming and a cheap building material if necessary.
Mycelium	The same use as grass and dirt, but only found on mushroom islands.
Sand	A beach biome ground that can be mixed with gunpowder to craft TNT or smelted to make glass.

PLANTS

Block	Use
Cactus	These blocks will hurt anything that contacts it. Can only grow in sand.
Grass	Perfect for farmland when tilled with a farm hoe.
Log	Can be crafted into wood planks and sticks to create a huge variety of different tools and items.
Melon, Pumpkin etc.	Fruit blocks are great for farming and have a wide variety of uses (including helmets, if you're in a silly, goofy mood.

LIQUIDS

Block	Use
Lava	Dangerous to encounter, but it can be used to create stone and obsidian.
Water	A key block needed for any budding farmer, aquatic pet owner, or putting out an unexpected fire.

STONE

Block	Use
Bedrock	An indestructible block that cannot be broken.
Clay	Can drop clay balls when mined.
Gravel	Can be used to suffocate mobs.
Obsidian	A rock with unbeatable explosion-resistance. Great for defensive builds. Required to build a nether portal.
Sandstone	Unlike sand, it is unaffected by gravity, so it is a good resource for building.

ORES AND MINERALS

Block	Use
Coal Ore	A common but very valuable ore for items like torches.
Diamond Ore	Can be mined for one of the game's most valuable resources for tools and armour.
Gold Ore	A rare ore that drops gold when mined with (at least) an iron pickaxe. Can also be smelted to create gold ingots.
Iron Ore	A common ore found around and below sea-level. This is a good resource for early game pickaxes.
Lapis Lazuli Ore	This ore can be used for dyes, decoration and enchantment.
Redstone Ore	Drops redstone when mined, a valuable resource for mechanical creations.

STRUCTURAL BLOCKS

Structural blocks can be found in generated structures, but they can still be used by the player. Finding structural blocks can be a blessing, as it's skipping a couple of steps compared to natural blocks.

Block	Use
Cobblestone	An excellent base construction material.
Farmland	These blocks can grow seeds into food resources.
Glass	Created by melting sand in a furnace, perfect for building features.
Mossy Cobblestone	A decorative variation of cobblestone.
Mossy Stonebrick	A decorative variation of stonebrick.
Stone Brick	A decorative block found in stronghold structures.
Wooden Plank	A super versatile block that is essential for crafting.
Wool	A block obtained from sheep that can be dyed.

NETHER BLOCKS

These blocks are found exclusively in the Nether. They're a tougher get, but some great resources.

Block	Use
Glowstone	A light source that can be found within the Nether.
Nether Brick	A strong building material from the Nether.
Netherrack	The stone of the Nether. Good resource for bonfires.
Soul Sand	This block slows the movement of whoever is on it. It's required to plant nether wart and summon the wither.

For more information on the Nether realm, check out The Three Dimensions on p. 22.

MICHELIN
MINECRAFT

If you're playing Minecraft in Survival mode, then you're going to have to get familiar with the game's culinary offerings. Just like real world survival, you have to eat to keep chugging along - and not all food fuels are made equal.

HUNGER

Hunger is represented by the ten little drumsticks on the right-hand side above your hotbar. You have a max total of 20 hunger points - so each drumstick represents 2 points each.

Your gameplay abilities depend on your hunger levels. Having 18+ hunger means your health will automatically regenerate. Sprinting isn't possible if your hunger points are below 6. And if your hunger hits 0? Then your health starts taking the hit until you chow something down.

KITCHEN KIT

When it comes to kitting out your kitchen, you're going to need to turn to the trusty crafting menu to rustle up some key pieces.
- **Crafting Table (wooden plank x3)**
- **Furnace (cobblestone x8)**
- **Boat (wooden plank x5)**
- **Bowl (wooden plank x3)**
- **Fishing Rod (sticks x3, string x2)**
- **Bone Meal (bone x1)**

Mob	Meat	Hunger (raw)	Hunger (Cooked)
Cow	Beef	+3	+8
Mooshroom			
Pig	Porkchop	+3	+8
Sheep	Mutton	+2	+6
Chicken	Chicken	+2 (30% food poisoning chance)	+6
Rabbit	Rabbit	+3	+5
Zombie	Rotten Flesh	+4 (80% food poisoning chance)	N/A

Desperate times call for desperate measures. If you need to eat something that can give you food poisoning, drink milk straight after eating to cure it.

FISH

Fish	Hunger Points (Raw)	Hunger Points (Cooked)
Fish	+2	+5
Salmon	+2	+6

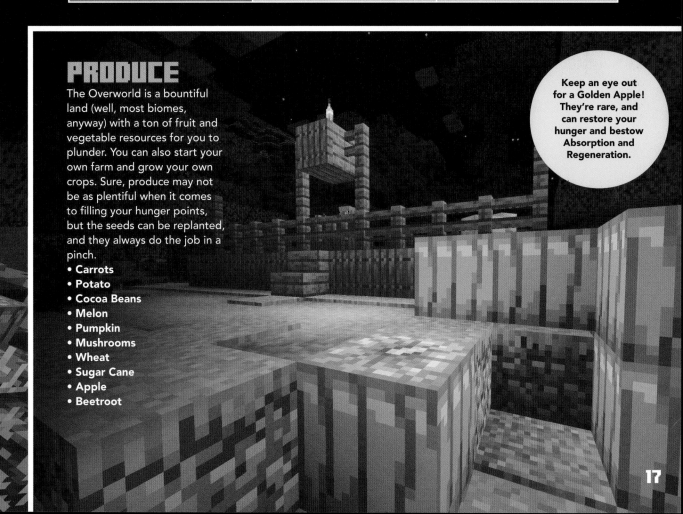

PRODUCE

The Overworld is a bountiful land (well, most biomes, anyway) with a ton of fruit and vegetable resources for you to plunder. You can also start your own farm and grow your own crops. Sure, produce may not be as plentiful when it comes to filling your hunger points, but the seeds can be replanted, and they always do the job in a pinch.

• Carrots
• Potato
• Cocoa Beans
• Melon
• Pumpkin
• Mushrooms
• Wheat
• Sugar Cane
• Apple
• Beetroot

Keep an eye out for a Golden Apple! They're rare, and can restore your hunger and bestow Absorption and Regeneration.

WELCOME TO THE OVERWORLD: BIOMES

The Overworld is the primary dimension of Minecraft, and is teeming with a wide variety of terrains known as biomes. Each biome has its own resources, mobs, and even environmental behaviours like weather cycles.

ARID LANDS

Arid land biomes never experience rain or snowfall, and are often covered in very sparse vegetation. These biomes can be further divided into three categories:

• **Deserts:** The desert is harsh and unforgiving, with a whole lot of sand, sandstone and the occasional cacti and pillager outpost.
• **Badlands:** This uncommon biome is usually the desert's neighbour, with red sand and large veins of glittering gold. Badlands aren't home to any passive mobs, but there are hostile ones in the abandoned
• **Savannas:** Savannas are flat and populated with acacia and small oak trees. Survival in a savanna biome is usually pretty ideal thanks to its wood sources and passive mobs like horses and llamas.

Biomes
Desert, Savanna, Savanna Plateau, Windswept Savanna, Badlands, Wooded Badlands, Eroded Badlands

CAVES

Cave biomes are there to lure you into a spot of casual underground exploration, but make sure you're well prepared before plunging into these unknown depths. Yes, the caves are full of amazing resources and long-lost treasures of ancient cities, but they're also home to lots of lava and some of the game's most dangerous mobs - shriekers and wardens.

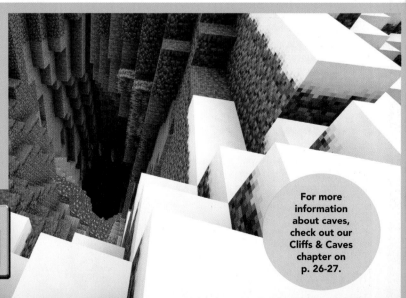

Biomes
Deep Dark, Dripstone Caves, Lush Caves

For more information about caves, check out our Cliffs & Caves chapter on p. 26-27.

FLATLANDS

Flatlands are, well, flat (it's all in the name, honestly) with fewer trees than the average grassland biome. These biomes can be further divided into two categories:

• **Plains:** These flat and grassy biomes are the best biome to find villages and settlements. These biomes are great to set up base due to docile farm mobs and horses that spawn here - and the wide open terrain makes spotting caves, waterfalls or bordering terrains super easy.

• **Snowy Plains:** Considerably less friendly than their regular variation, these biomes are hard to survive in. Rabbits and polar bears are known to spawn here, but it is also home to hostile strays.

Biomes
Plains, Sunflower Plains, Snowy Plains, Ice Spikes

HIGHLANDS

You'll find highland biomes up high on the Y-axis. While they may share a similar altitude, there is a wide variety of ecosystems up there, which can largely be divided into two categories:

• **Mountains**: Mountains are rarer biomes that can further be sorted into either peaks or slopes. While peaks are rather unforgiving and difficult to cross, slopes (including meadows and cherry groves) are friendlier, more peaceful biomes with some unique resources up for grabs.

• **Windswept Hills:** These biomes have unique features such as floating blocks and islands. They also boast a lot of great viewpoints, like large waterfalls and overhangs. While they may be pretty, they're not super survival-friendly; water must be covered to prevent it freezing, and there's always the risk of fall damage from up in those heights.

Highland biomes are the only places you can find emerald ore.

Biomes
Jagged Peaks, Frozen Peaks, Stony Peaks, Meadow, Cherry Grove, Grove, Snowy Slopes, Windswept Hills, Windswept Gravelly Hills, Windswept Forest

WETLANDS

Wetland biomes are great resources for water. These biomes can be sorted into three categories:

• **Rivers:** Rivers serve as borders between different biomes. You can usually find seagrass or sugar cane along the riverbed and bank, and salmon and squid beneath the water's surface.

• **Swamps:** Swamps can be pretty dangerous, with witches, slimes and drowned mobs ready to pounce. If you're looking for a challenge, it's a great place to start a slime farm.

• **Beaches:** These biomes generate whenever another biome meets the ocean, which means its variation depends on the surrounding terrains.

Biomes

River, Frozen River, Swamp, Mangrove Swamp, Beach, Snowy Beach, Stony Shore

WOODLANDS

Woodlands are rich in plant-based resources, and have the most varieties of all the biomes. You can generally sort these terrains into three categories:

• **Forests:** Forests are great for harvesting whatever wood you need, with a lot of different wood types and colours to choose from. Dark forests are a little more dangerous, as the lack of light means more dangerous mobs spawn there.

• **Jungles:** These forested biomes are full of tall trees and vines, as well as more unique structures like jungle temples. It's also rich with good food resources such as melons and cocoa pods.

• **Taigas:** Taigas are hilly cross-biomes between jungles and forests. You'll find more spruce trees and ferns here instead of the usual oaks and birches you'd find in forests.

Biomes

Forest, Flower Forest, Taiga, Old Growth Pine Taiga, Old Growth Spruce Taiga, Snowy Taiga, Birch Forest, Old Growth Birch Forest, Dark Forest, Jungle, Sparse Jungle, Bamboo Jungle

OCEANS AND DEEP OCEANS

The ocean is a vast beast, covering around 25-33% of the Overworld's surface area. And it goes as deep as it does wide, too, with sea level clocking in at Y=63 and the ocean floor at around Y=45. Mob spawning depends on the depth and temperature of the variant biomes. You'll also find shipwrecks and monuments beneath the surface.

Biomes

Ocean, Warm Ocean, Lukewarm Ocean, Cold Ocean, Frozen Ocean, Deep Ocean, Deep Lukewarm Ocean, Deep Cold Ocean, Deep Frozen Ocean

MUSHROOM FIELDS

Mushroom Fields are a super rare biome that can spawn right in the middle of the ocean. This island biome is covered in mycelium (a very rare resource) and brown and red mushrooms. It's the only biome where mooshrooms naturally spawn, and isn't home to any hostile mobs, so if you manage to come across one, it's a pretty good place to call home.

Biomes

N/A

Try using a boat or elytra glider to scout for Mushroom Fields.

THE THREE DIMENSIONS

The world of Minecraft is split into three realms: the Overworld, the Nether and the End. Each realm has its own unique biomes, resources and native mobs - both friendly and alarmingly hostile. Fancy a touch of interdimensional travel? Well, it's best to know what's in store before you start realm-hopping.

THE OVERWORLD

This is the default Minecraft world, where players can spend many-a-days quite happily without even a thought for another dimension. This realm is the most diverse and has the widest variety of different biomes and mobs, including friendly villages and settlements.

Biomes
Check out The World of Minecraft: Biomes on p.18-21.

THE NETHER

The Nether is a dangerous hellscape filled with lava seas, fire and a lot of fire-proof mobs that prefer the taste of you to the fungal vegetation on offer. Players have to create a nether portal out of obsidian in the Overworld in order to reach the Nether.

Biomes
Crimson Forest, Warped Forest, Nether Waste, Basalt Deltas, Soul Sand Valley

THE END

The End is a space-like dimension made up of floating end stone islands. This barren environment might not look like much, but it is home to some of the rarest items and mobs in Minecraft, like the elytra and the Ender Dragon. To reach the End, players must find a stronghold with eyes of ender and activate the portal.

Biomes
The End, Small End Islands, End Midlands, End Highlands, End Barrens

TRAILS AND TALES

Minecraft has always been a great canvas for storytellers, and the latest update - Trails & Tales - gives the player even more tools to craft their adventure and bring your stories to life!

Camels are ideal for traveling across more treacherous areas, as their long legs keep you out of reach of any melee mobs.

EXPRESS YOURSELF

This update focuses on creativity and self-expression, so there are a ton of new decorative blocks, resources and customization options to let you really make each of your Minecraft adventures your own.

WHAT'S NEW?

Trails & Tales comes with two new building blocks: bamboo and cherry. Players can travel the world on the back of a camel, and maybe even come across the beautiful but rare new biome, Cherry Grove.

Now we can discover secrets of the Minecraft world's past by indulging in a cheeky spot of archaeology to find ancient plants, pottery sherds (not a typo; you'll see soon enough) and sniffer eggs. Who needs Jurassic Park when you can find your very own previously-extinct sniffler and explore buried ruins with your brand new brush?

TELL YOUR STORY

But what's an adventure if no one ever hears of it? That's where the new library feature comes in, where players can craft stories in books and keep them safe in their very distinguished new bookshelf-lined libraries (and thanks to the new mob heads, silence is very much optional).

THE WILD

Things got real wild (heh) in the world of Minecraft with the Wild update in summer 2022. In fact, they got more than wild - they got a little dark and a little creepy, to be honest. Here are some changes one of the most major updates the game has seen since release brought to Minecraft.

NEW CREATURES

The creeper got a new big bad competing for the Least Desired Late Night Encounter Award, and the warden is certainly a tough competitor. This hideous mob slithers around deep dark biomes, and is summoned by sculk shriekers. Watch out - it deals the highest melee damage of all the mobs in the whole game. Their only weakness is their blindness, so players can evade them via sneaking, diversions and a quick prayer.

Thankfully the update brought some friendlier company to the Overworld, too. Frogs and tadpoles finally found their way to the swampland biomes. The update also introduced one of the more unique mobs in the game: the allay, a flying passive mob that can collect and deliver items for the player.

For more information on these new additions, as well as all the other mobs in the game, check out our chapter Mobs of Minecraft on p. 42-45.

NEW BIOMES

The Wild brought us the deep dark biome and the mangrove, the perfect dark, uncomfortably moist kind of environments for all the new creatures and existing crawlies to call home.

Deep Dark: This new cave biome is home to the terrifying warden mob, but with palatial ancient cities harboring chests with some of the rarest items in-game, the descent is worth the risk.

Mangrove Swamp: This variant of the swamp biome can be found in warmer regions (usually near jungles and deserts). It should be no surprise that these biomes are densely populated with mangrove trees.

NEW RESOURCES

Of course, new biomes generally mean new resources, with new blocks including sculk, mangrove wood and mud. These decorative blocks look great paired with froglights, new bright light-emitting decorative pieces made when a frog eats a magma cube (which isn't as horrifying as it initially sounds, trust me).

NEW ITEMS

The update also finally brought to us the partnership we've all been waiting for: boats and chests. Okay, wait, hear me out…

Joking aside, this perhaps previously unconsidered pairing is actually super useful. Adding a chest to a boat allows you to store more items with you on your travels, and ultimately encourages more Overworld exploration by making it a lot easier to prepare for your water-based trips. Sure, you might not have known you needed it, but it's the kind of thing you wonder how you survived without.

CAVES AND CLIFFS

Caves & Cliffs was one of the biggest and most ambitious updates that Mojang brought to Minecraft since its release. Sure, skins and mobs are cute, but this update totally opened up the world of exploration like no other. It truly put the mine in Minecraft.

MY MINING KIT

So you're ready to answer the siren call of the dark unknown? You never know what you might find in there, but you can at least be sure you're prepared for the journey. Make sure you've got these mining essentials packed:

• **Torches:** Goes without saying at this point, but we'll say it anyway - don't forget your light sources!
• **Wood:** You might need to make a cheeky craft table or chest if you make a rest point, and trust, you won't be finding any wood down there.
• **Food:** Mining is a dangerous business with a lot of possibility for unexpected damage, so keep food on you to mitigate any of that.
• **Tools:** Always bring back-up pickaxes or shovels. It's better to be with extra than without.
• **Weapons:** There are a lot of nasties lurking in the dark that haven't seen a good meal in a while. Be ready to defend yourself if necessary.
• **Bucket:** This is optional, but it's useful for collecting water or lava if you need it.

Want to make the most of cave exploration? Be sure to turn on your coordinates so you know where you're at. Console players can find them on the map, and desktop players can find them in the debug menu with F3.

FINDING ORE

Caves are home to some of the game's most useful and valuable ores. Whether you're looking for a gear upgrade, fuel for enchantment or even a solid gold wall for your home (hey, do you), you'll likely find the ore you need in the darkness of a cave. Use this chart to approximate where you're more likely to find specific ores. You're welcome.

When it comes to mining, always do it in a diagonal direction. Mining directly downwards could open you up to a deathly drop into a pool of lava or on top of a bloodthirsty mob. Mining directly upwards could open up a little trapdoor for a bunch of lava to fall on your head, or a loose block like sand or gravel falling down and suffocating you. Be safe! Diagonal movement is your friend.

Ore	Location	Note
Coal	Y=0 to Y=256	The most optimal spawn point for Coal is around Y=90.
Copper	Y=-16 to Y=-112	You're likely to find Copper in the Dripstone Cave biome, around Y=48.
Diamond	Y=-64 to Y=16	Diamonds are more likely to spawn the lower down you dig.
Emerald	Y=-16 to Y=236	Unlike most other ores, Emeralds are more likely to spawn overground, at a height of Y=224.
Gold	Y=-64 to Y-32	Gold generates at Y=-16, but at low quantities. You're actually better off looking in the Nether for gold, as it spawns more often there.
Iron	Y=-32 to Y=256	The range for iron is so wide because it's a very commonly found ore.
Lapis Lazuli	Y=-64 to Y=64	Lapis Lazuli is super rare, but can more likely be found at Y=0.
Redstone	Y=-64 to Y=-32	The lower you go, the more likely you'll come across Redstone.

WHERE ARE STEVE AND ALEX?

Help! Steve and Alex went off on another whirlwind adventure to add another tome to their ever-expanding adventure library - but they seem to have gotten a bit lost this time! Can you spot them? Answer on p. 62-63.

FIRST DAY ESSENTIALS

Congrats on reading up on the world and its resources - are you ready to put that to the test? Minecraft is a pretty daunting game in that the game begins as soon as you spawn in, and it's not going to give you any tutorials as to how to learn anything. Learning by experience is Mojang's method of choice, but a little bit of prep for your first steps won't hurt. Here's a guide to your first 24 hours of survival to set you up for success.

Can't find anywhere to settle down? You might have gotten dealt a bad hand by the spawn gods. No worries, you can just quit out and restart a new game for a more favourable spawn location. There's no shame in it - even Bear Grylls-adjacent adventurers can only do so much with rough beginnings.

THE FIRST DAY

1 **Find wood.** As soon as you spawn in, you'll want to start gathering some wood. Any type of wood will do, you just need enough to get started with some key tools and structures.

2 **Find a suitable shelter spot.** You need to start looking for somewhere to set up a temporary base as soon as possible. Ideally, you should be aiming for a nice open area with access to wood, water, and some food resources nearby.

3 **Craft a pickaxe.** Your pickaxe is your first port of call when it comes to crafting, so once you have enough wood (14-15 logs will get the job done), open up your inventory and use the logs in the crafting menu to create planks, then from planks, make the crafting table. Set up the crafting table and make your pickaxe.

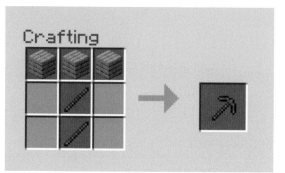

4 **Get mining.** With our pickaxe in hand, it's time to go after some tougher resources to make our tools a bit more durable. Keep an eye out for stone, and if you're mining down to get some, be sure to keep an exit route to ground level.

5 **Hunt down some resources.** It's time to fill out that inventory, so seek out your basic resources, like wood, stone and meat. Keep an eye on the sun while doing so, and try not to stray too far from your base.

6 **Set up shelter.** Our Day 1 abode doesn't have to be anything too fancy. You have two options depending on how well your resource hunting went - you can either set up a little shack with four walls, or dig down and make a little cove at the end of a tunnel for you to hunker down in.

7 **Make torches.** With the stone you hopefully gathered during the day, make a furnace to make some torches. Light is the best way to keep yourself safe during the night, so make as many as you can - light up your shelter and keep some on hand for a little night wandering too.

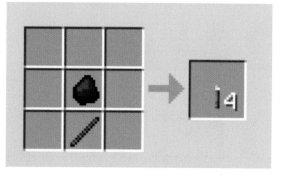

THE FIRST NIGHT

Keep gathering for tomorrow. I hope you didn't think night time was time to rest. Maybe in a few days when we have a bed, but this is the first day, baby - we're doing an all nighter. With your home lit up and your torches in hand, it's time to mine around your base to boost up your resources. You might even come across some great early game ores like iron and coal.

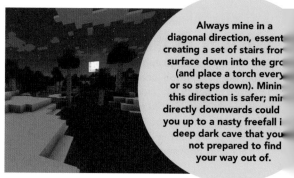

Always mine in a diagonal direction, essent creating a set of stairs fror surface down into the gr (and place a torch ever or so steps down). Minin this direction is safer; min directly downwards could you up to a nasty freefall i deep dark cave that you not prepared to find your way out of.

THE NEXT DAY

And with the sunrise, you should be all set to start your adventure with a well-stocked inventory. Go for the world's longest walk, start seeking out landmarks or even start building your dream home on the spot if you lucked out finding a good plot of land. You survived your first day (and night), it all begins from here...

HOME SWEET HOME

A homebase is a key point to any successful adventure. Having somewhere to return and kick off your enchanted golden boots is way more important that you'd think.

Look, I get it, Minecraft is all about exploration, and you probably just want to climb to the top of that mountain, dive to the bottom of that cave and fly across that swamp to see what's waiting for you. You've probably got a lot of questions, like…

WHY SHOULD I BUILD A HOME?

Sure, being on-the-go and discovering new things is fun, but every good adventurer has somewhere to return to eventually. Homes in Minecraft provide a safe space from hostile mobs, a great storage location for all those spoils from your travels, and the best way to lay out the (literal, in some cases) seeds for your long-term survival.

WELL, WHERE SHOULD I BUILD A HOME?

The 'perfect spot' for building a home isn't a black-and-white answer. Where you decide to put down some roots depends on what you're looking for in terms of gameplay. Some people like a nice and chill vibe in the flower field, while others might prefer a beachfront property or snowy mountain experience. Whatever your preference, you'll want to look for somewhere that meets the following criteria:
• Decent proximity to sources of wood, food and other common items (like ores).
• Close enough to water (river or ocean) for fast travel.
• A little bit of altitude so you can get the advantage on any hostile mobs that come visit.
• And of course, enough open area to accommodate your house plans.

OKAY, BUT HOW DO I BUILD A HOME?

Again, it depends on what kind of features you personally would like for your home, but there is a basic kind of checklist you can go through when building:

1 **Build your walls.** Nice and easy, just a basic four will do, with spaces for doors and windows left in advance. You'll want to go for a good solid block, like some kind of stone, that isn't flammable.

2 **Add doors and windows.** Leaving open spaces is functional, sure, but invites mobs like skeletons to shoot an arrow through it, or worse, walk right in while you're sleeping. Craft doors and glass to keep your place secure.

3 **Expand.** With this basic structure in place, you can build up (or out, or down) from there. Add some practical elements like a roof, for sure, but from there, you can add more rooms, additional floors etc. (don't forget to add ladders or stairs if you're doing another floor).

4 **Add lights.** Light is the one thing that protects you from some of the hostile nasties of the game, so safeguard your home by adding some form of light, be it torches or something more aesthetic like froglights or glowstone.

5 With the basics done, you can now focus on **adding some amenities like furniture.** Your first priority should be a bed in order to set a spawn point, but also consider some chests, a crafting table, and some food source (like a basic farm).

Why not consider a pet to make it really homey? Try taming an ocelot or cat with raw fish - they're great to ward off creepers and keep your home a little bit safer.

KNOW YOUR INVENTORY

It travels with you wherever you go, and is long often neglected when it comes to strategy: your inventory.

You're bound to collect a whole plethora of items - both made and discovered - on your adventures across the three realms, but throwing everything you find into your bag without a second thought is a recipe for disaster, especially if you're serious about gathering ingredients and resources for some of the game's more complex recipes.

Keeping things tidy is no one's idea of fun, but a little inventory management never hurt anyone. In a game as resource-oriented as Minecraft, you should make a point to keep on top of your items and available space so you're never caught in a pinch, wishing you hadn't left something in your chest at home.

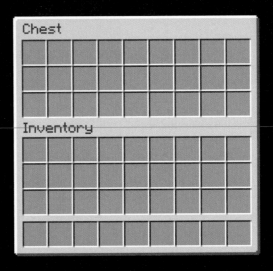

INVENTORY MANAGEMENT

Your inventory is what you carry with you at all times, so you need to make sure you've prepared the best items with you for whatever adventure lies ahead that day. With 27 slots available, consider separating them out into the following categories to cover your bases:

• **Tools (2 slots)** - You'll only ever need a max of two tool types: one for main use and a niche pick, just in case you come across something fancy.

• **Crafting Utilities (4 slots)** - Who knows what you'll need to whip on a whim? Best use these four slots to carry crafting utilities like crafting tables, furnaces, etc.

• **Weapons (2 slots)** - Two weapon types should be all you need, and stacking them up with spares is always a good idea.

• **Lighting (1 slot)** - You should never be without some form of emergency light source, like a stack of torches.

• **Food (1 slot)** - No need to pack a whole picnic, but a stack of cooked meat will get the job done when you need to top up your hunger bar.

• **Potions (4 slots)** - This is a late-game kinda deal, and the type of potions you carry depend on your particular play style preference. Fire Resistance and Night Vision are always good emergency potions to carry on you.

• **General (6 slots)** - You'll likely need resources for whatever you're up to, like wood, or a ladder, etc.

• **Free (7 slots)** - The final slots are free for whatever you need (if you still need anything) for your day's goal. Out foraging? Keep them open. Building a new floor to your home? Load them up with sand and stone. Whatever you require.

STORAGE

• Whatever you don't need to hand, you should be keeping in storage. That's where chests come in. While one will likely do at the start of the game, you'll need some more sophisticated storage

• Build a room in your home that's dedicated just to chests. That way, everything is one place and it's a one stop shop to get whatever you need.

• Consider categorising your storage if you have a lot of different items. You can have one chest for combat items, one for armour, one for tools etc.

CRAFTING

You can't spell Minecraft without 'craft' - and you can't expect to survive without mastering the game's crafting system. Whether you're after an end crystal or literal wooden stick, you're going to have to master the craft.

THE CRAFTING GRID

Crafting is a grid-based system. Players always have access to a 2x2 grid in their inventory, which allows players to craft simple recipes quickly on the go. For more complex (and the vast majority of) recipes, players can use a larger 3x3 grid by using a crafting table.

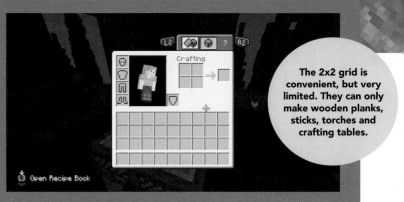

The 2x2 grid is convenient, but very limited. They can only make wooden planks, sticks, torches and crafting tables.

CRAFTING RECIPES

The Recipe Book is a super useful resource that is home to all of the possible crafting recipes, including recipes for other processes like smelting and brewing.

You can unlock recipes throughout the game by doing lots of different things, like gathering new materials or even just walking across a biome. Exploration is a great way to discover new things, but if you want a shortcut, try using a knowledge book.

Need recipe info, stat? There are plenty of great online catalogs that have interactive crafting grids. Try www.minecraft-crafting.net to find out how to craft any item in the game.

MASTER YOUR CRAFT

Fancy yourself a master crafter? There are a ton of resources out there to leaf through to find the perfect craft, but a true Minecraft maestro has the most useful recipes on the tips of their fingertips. Do you know what combining the ingredients below can make?

Check out p. 62-63 for answers.

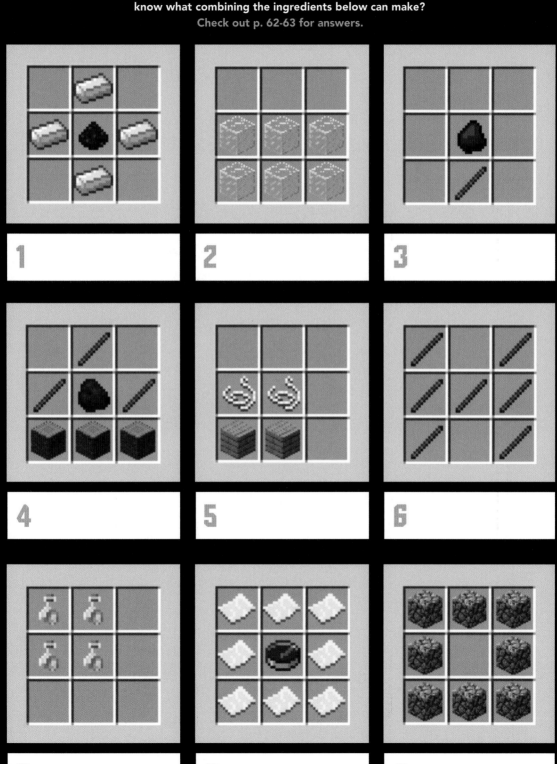

1

2

3

4

5

6

7

8

9

MINECRAFT MINERAL MIX-UP

Can you unscramble these Minecraft minerals? Don't worry - we've given you the first letter of each word as a hint! Check out the answers on p. 62-63.

1 IORN

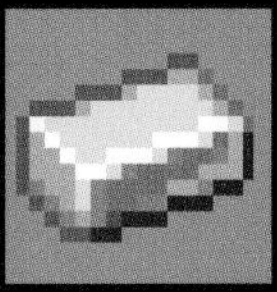

2 DDMAION

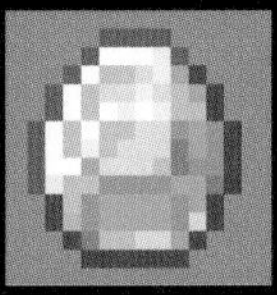

3 GLOD

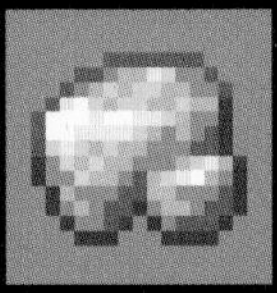

4 ATHTYSEM

5 EADLERM

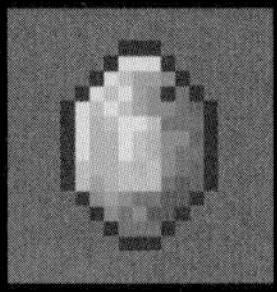

6 LPIAS LZULIA

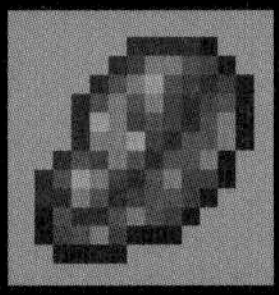

7 ODIIABSN

8 CLOA

9 CPREPO

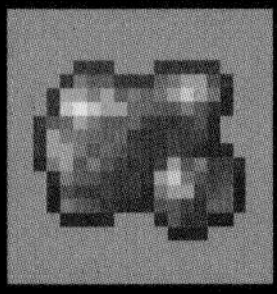

ENCHANTING

When it gets to mid-to-late gameplay, you're ready for something a bit more advanced than just crafting or smelting. Something a bit more risky. Something a bit more… magical?

Enchanting allows you to augment your equipment with some really powerful magical buffs, but it comes with the possibility of totally losing the item in the process. Ready to take the risk?

GETTING STARTED

If you want to enchant items, first things first, you'll need an enchanting table. To craft one, you'll need four obsidians, two diamonds and one book. With the table made, you'll have to exchange lapis lazuli and XP in order to fuel the process.

There's also a chance to come across enchanted items during regular gameplay. There's a chance to get some by trading emeralds with villagers or piglins, getting a lucky drop from some higher risk mobs, looting from the End City, or even just a lucky fishing trip.

ENHANCING YOUR ENCHANTMENTS

The higher your experience level, the better your enchantments, so get to practising. You can also boost your enchantment chances by setting up your enchanting table near some bookshelves - you can put up to 15 to get the maximum bookshelf buff.

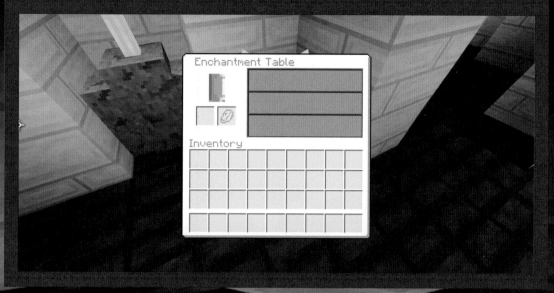

THE BEST ENCHANTMENTS

There are around thirty different types of enchantment to choose from and different rankings within each type. It can be quite intimidating to work out where to start, and the process isn't cheap enough to just be throwing lapis lazuli and XP around to find out what's best. So to save you the time, here are some enchantments that are worth prioritising over the others:

• **Mending (I):** This enchantment is super useful because regardless of your power or experience, you'll always be hampered by wear and tear, especially if your gear's higher-end. Mending gives XP bubbles the ability to repair, so you can fix up your weapons after using them.

• **Efficiency (I-V)/Fortune (I):** Resource gathering just got a whole lot luckier when your tools are augmented with these enchantments. Efficiency increases your mining speed and Fortune increases the amount of drops.

• **Sharpness (I-V)/Power (I-V):** These augments are perfect for weapons to boost your overall power. There are other offensive enchantments (like Piercing or Channelling), but as they're more specific, Sharpness/Power is the better option if you don't want to have to carry specific weapons around.

• **Protection (I-IV):** Protection is a very general augment that lessens damage from a broad range of sources. There are other defensive augments, but they're more specific in application, which could leave you vulnerable.

• **Feather Falling (I-IV):** If you're sick of losing your life after losing your footing every time you go hiking, put this enchantment on your boots to lessen fall damage.

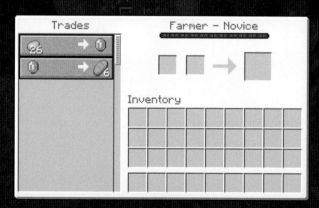

MOBS OF MINECRAFT

Even if you're playing single player, you're never alone in the world of Minecraft. All three realms are teeming with life - teeming with mobs, to be exact. Mobs (short for 'mobile entity') are living creatures - friends and foes, monsters and humans - that populate the same space as you. There are a whole load of different types out there, but they can largely be classed into four categories.

PASSIVE MOBS

These mobs are harmless and more than happy to coexist - they won't even attack back if you strike them. Most of them have a useful drop for the player if killed, but some of them have other uses, like providing transport or makeshift home security.

Mob	Info	Mob	Info
Allay	Can search out items in the world for you.	Parrot	Can be tamed and detect hostile mobs within 20 blocks.
Axolotl	Can follow you into battle underwater.	Pig	Useful drops include pork chops.
Bat	N/A	Pufferfish	Useful drops include bonemeal.
Camel	Can be ridden by two players.	Rabbit	Useful drops include rabbit hide, raw rabbit and rabbit's foot.
Cat	Can be tamed and ward off phantoms and creepers.	Salmon	Useful drops include raw salmon.
Chicken	Useful drops include feathers and raw chicken.	Sheep	Useful drops include wool and mutton.
Cod	Useful drops include raw cod and bonemeal.	Skeleton horse	Can be tamed if their rider is killed. The fastest method of transport in game.
Cow	Useful drops include leather and raw beef.	Sniffer	Can only be hatched from a sniffer egg. Sniffs out seeds from the ground.
Donkey	Can be ridden as a method of transportation (with an inventory).	Snow golem	Can also be spawned by an enderman.
Fox	If bred, they will defend the player against mobs.	Squid	Useful drops include ink sacs.
Frog	Drops froglights after eating magma cubes.	Strider	Drops string. Can be ridden.
Glow squid	Useful drops include glow ink sacs.	Tadpole	Grow into frogs.
Horse	Can be ridden as a method of transportation (with an inventory).	Tropical fish	Useful drops include tropical fish and bonemeal.
Mooshroom	Useful drops include leather and raw beef.	Turtle	Useful drops include sea grass.
Mule	Can be ridden as a method of transportation (with an inventory).	Villager	Useful for trading and other services.
Ocelot	Can be tamed and ward off phantoms and creepers.	Wandering trader	Useful drops include milk bucket.

NEUTRAL MOBS

Neutral mobs will leave you alone... Unless you strike them first. Then they'll make it their business to fight back.

Mob	Info	Mob	Info
Bee	Can be farmed to collect honey and honeycomb.	Panda	Useful drops include bamboo.
Cave spider	Useful drops include string and spider eye.	Piglin	Will drop whatever it is holding.
Dolphin	Useful drops include raw cod.	Polar bear	Useful drops include raw cod and raw salmon.
Enderman	Useful drops include ender pearls.	Spider	Useful drops include string and spider eye.
Goat	Useful drops include goat horns.	Trader llama	Can be equipped with a chest for mobile inventory.
Iron golem	Killing a village Iron Golem lowers the player's village popularity by 10.	Wolf	Can be tamed and help the player in battle.
Llama	Can be equipped with a chest for mobile inventory.	Zombified piglin	Useful drops include gold nuggets and gold ingots.

HOSTILE MOBS

It's best to steer clear of these mobs unless you are prepared to fight, because it is on sight with these things. Hostile mobs will spring to attack as soon as the player steps within their detection range, which can go from the usual 16 blocks to 100 blocks. Don't be too avoidant, though - their drops are some of the most useful items in game.

Mob	Useful Drops	Mob	Useful Drops
Blaze	Blaze rod	Shulker	Shulker shell
Chicken jockey	N/A	Silverfish	N/A
Creeper	Gunpowder	Skeleton	Bone, Arrow
Drowned	Copper ingot, Trident	Skeleton horseman	
Elder guardian	Prismarine shard, Wet sponge, Raw cod	Slime	Slimeball
Endermite	N/A	Spider jockey	N/A
Evoker	Totem of undying, Emerald, Ominous banner	Stray	Bone, Arrow, Arrow of slowness
Ghast	Ghast tear, Gunpowder	Vex	N/A
Guardian	Raw cod, Prismarine crystal	Vindicator	Emerald, Ominous banner, Iron axe
Hoglin	Raw pork chop, Leather	Warden	Sculk catalyst
Husk	Iron ingot	Witch	Glass bottle, Glowstone dust, Gunpowder, Redstone, Spider eye, Sugar
Magma cube	Magma cream	Wither skeleton	Bone, Coal, Wither skeleton skull, Sword
Phantom	Phantom membrane	Zoglin	N/A
Piglin brute	Golden axe	Zombie	Iron ingot
Pillager	Crossbow, Ominous banner	Zombie villager	Iron ingot
Ravager	Saddle		

BOSS MOBS

Think of boss mobs like evolved hostile mobs. Final form hostile mobs, if you will. Comparatively, boss mobs have a mammoth amount of health, a much larger detection range and a much stronger bloodlust. Taking on a boss mob is the game's ultimate test of skill. There are only two in game:
• The **wither** can be summoned by the player. It drops 50XP and a nether star. When it takes damage, it breaks all blocks within a 3x4x3 radius (and is the only mob capable of destroying Obsidian).
• The **ender dragon** can be found within the End realm. It is immune to all status effects. Defeating the ender dragon grants the player a dragon egg

MINECRAFT WORDSEARCH

Any explorer worth their blocks has a keen eye on them, especially when roaming the open (and often openly hostile, let's be honest) plains of the overworld. Put that eye to the test and see if you can spot things you should be looking out for on your travels in the wordsearch below.

Check out p. 62-63 for answers.

```
W H Y M C D H E T C W K O D M
W S M S X U N F M J M I N S V
Y Z F L Z N W H V S J A F B A
Q M X R D G D A T P L N E X N
E Q I C O E K R O S H D M I O
I D W N N O O R I N R D U P F
T D O W E N X G Z O M B I E S
E R O E G S N D C P F R L J W
U R A H G I H K L C Y L E E B
D L O D T E G A L L I V C A H
L L A A E O O N F Q K Y Y M W
D Y O B M R L S Y T A G M A V
R L R U I N E D P O R T A L V
F C I T T H M I X Z Q K R L H
E N D E R D R A G O N F R B I
```

Floating Island   Village   Golem
Ruined Portal   **Geode**   **Bedrock**
Mineshaft   Llama   Ore
Dungeon   **Drowned**   **Mycelium**
Stronghold   Zombie   Ender Dragon
              Trader

SURVIVAL TIPS

Want the TL;DR version of surviving in Minecraft? Just keep these tips as your foundation and you should be good.

BE PREPARED

Danger is always looking to take you by surprise in Survival mode, and while you can't avoid it completely, you can ensure you're ready to deal with it. Always be prepared - that's carrying some torches, some food resources and a back-up weapon with you before you start mining.

DEFENCE OVER OFFENCE

Don't just go into any fight with your sword a-swingin', remember to prioritise keeping your health high and avoiding damage... then get your strikes in safely. The same mindset goes for protecting your home - the game has a bunch of traps and security systems you can use to keep mobs away, so use them.

LISTEN FOR DANGER

If you're finding it hard to hear approaching mobs sneaking up on you over your own footsteps, then open up the audio settings. Player footsteps and mob footsteps are classified as separate sounds, so you can bring the player footsteps audio down in order to single out mob footsteps.

BETTER WITH MOBS

Make use of friendly mobs to enhance your gameplay. Wolves can make great company for travelling if you find yourself in an unexpected fight, and Ocelots and Cats are great home pets to ward off Creepers.

DON'T BE AFRAID TO FLEE

Fleeing isn't cowardly, it's a smart tactical decision that even the best players have to make. If the battle looks overwhelming, then step away - you don't always have to engage and fight to the death.

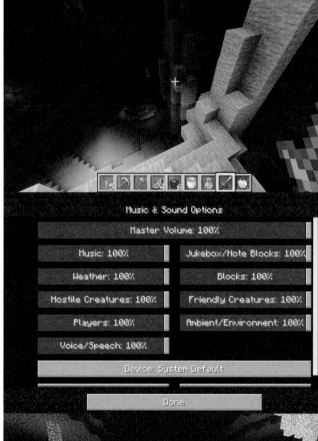

COMBAT

So the game isn't called Combatcraft, or Minecombat, but combat is still a big component of Minecraft - maybe second to mining and crafting. You'd be hard pressed to try to survive without needing to engage in combat, from hunting down mobs for specific drops, accidentally stumbling across something (or someone) hostile and ready to swing, or even going after the game's ultimate boss, the ender dragon.

WEAPONS
There are four weapon types in the game: swords, tridents, bows and crossbows. Axes technically fall under tools, but they can also be used offensively.

SHORT-RANGE COMBAT
• Swords and axes
Most combat engagements are short-range, whether you're the initiator or you've been sprung. In short-range combat, you'll always want to try to find higher ground, even if it's only one block up. The high ground advantage is universal across pretty much all video games, and Minecraft is no exception.

LONG-RANGE COMBAT
• Bows and arrows
Certain foes are worth being held at a distance, so it's best to invest in a good bow. The distance of the shot, impact power and inflicted damage all depend on how hard you pull back on the bow. Minecraft bows use real-world flight physics, so arrows lose velocity the further they travel. Translated? You're not Hawkeye - don't go so long-range that the arrow loses all force before it even reaches the target.

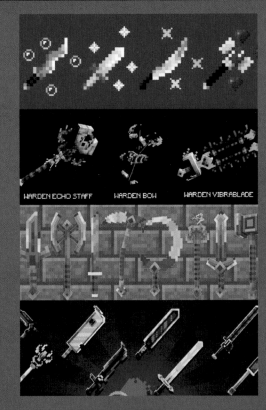

WARDEN ECHO STAFF   WARDEN BOW   WARDEN VIBRABLADE

Timing is everything! Don't just blindly strike your opponent over and over. Try to time your attack for when your enemy is just about to strike you. If you manage to interrupt their attack, it gives you a window to reposition.

ARMOUR

The best offence is a good defence, so armour is a must for any adventurer. Even if you don't have any intentions of getting into fights, you should still suit up just in case you fall victim to a rogue creeper explosion. You can craft the most basic of armour with 24 iron ingots, but you can also usually snag a set from chests in villages (hey, finders keepers).

SHIELDS

Blocking incoming hits is just as good as landing them in the larger combat equation (you know, where the intended outcome is your survival). Sure, it's an optional addition to your gear rollout, but it can absorb incoming damage and protect against explosions. To craft one, use 6 wood planks (any kind of wood will do) and 1 iron ingot. You can add a banner to a completed shield to create a patterned shield.

49

TEST YOUR KNOWLEDGE

Alright, so you've spent 50 pages absorbing all of this invaluable, expert advice we have imparted upon you - how much did you really take in? Let's test your Minecraft knowledge, and see whether you can call yourself a Minecraft Master and complete this mega quiz! **Check out p. 62-63 for answers.**

1 What are the names of Minecraft's two most popular characters?

2 What's the name of Minecraft's foundational rock?

3 Which block do you need to create a nether portal?

4 How many sticks do you need to craft a sword?

5 Which resource do you need to fuel enchanting?

6 Which mob can be tamed if you kill its rider?

7 Which biome are you most likely to find copper in?

8 What potion can help you see in the dark?

9 How many dimensions are there?

10 Which enchantment lessens fall damage?

11 What mob can find items for you?

12 Which food has the highest hunger points?

13 What's the name of the dirt found only on mushroom islands?

14 How many diamonds do you need to make an enchantment table?

15 What do you get for defeating the ender dragon?

16 What mob does a sculk shrieker summon?

17 Which ore is more likely to spawn at extreme heights?

18 What is the best potion for dealing with lava?

19 What are creepers afraid of?

20 What should you do if you have food poisoning?

21 Which fish is poisonous to eat?

22 Which ore can be used to create machines?

23 Where can you find a Mooshroom?

24 Which item increases your chances of successful enchantment?

25 What mob can detect seeds in the ground for you?

MINECRAFT MAZE

Looks like Steve forgot his compass looking for gold in the badlands. Can you help him find his gold and his way out of the mines? Check out p. 62-63 for answers.

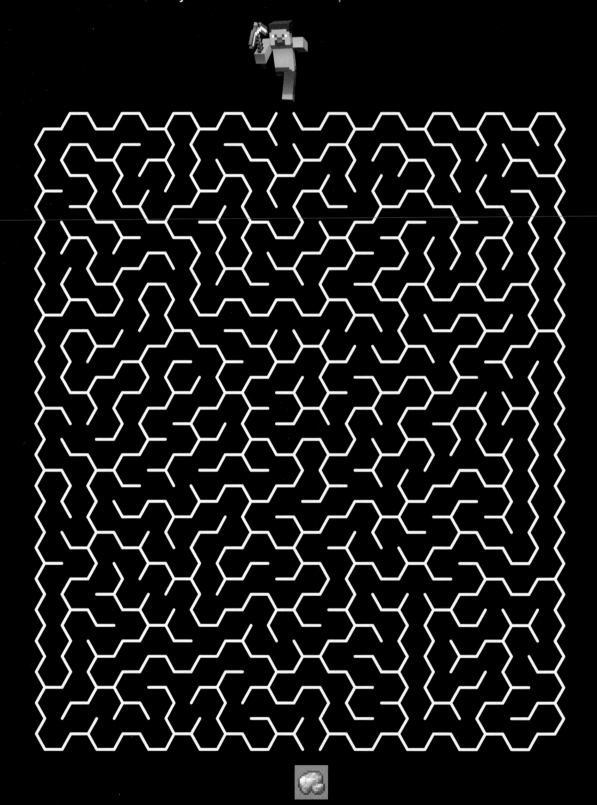

COMMAND CENTRE

As we well know by now, Minecraft is mammoth. Sometimes you want a little shortcut to tailor your adventure without having to put in all of those hours and risking it all by the whim of a shulker. That's where commands come in. "Cheat codes" sounds a little harsh - it's not cheating, per se, just a helping hand to steer things in the right direction. There are over 100 different commands in Minecraft, so obviously you're not going to need all of them. Here are some useful ones you might want to try out.

Command	Effect
/tp or /teleport	Give your feet a rest and teleport across the Minecraft world with a few keyboard taps. Just type your desired coordinates after the command and poof! You're there.
/gamemode	Change your game mode without having to leave your current world. Just type the mode you want to switch to (ex. /gamemode creative) to change.
/summon	Summon any entity with the /summon command. Want to see a warden? I mean… it's your funeral, dude, but sure, go ahead.
/locate	If you want to hunt for gold in the badlands without praying to the RNG gods to find one, this command is for you. Simply type /locate and the biome type or structure you want to find to get its coordinates, which you can then use /tp to teleport to.
/kill	Look, sometimes combat can be all just a bit too much. We've all been there. This command lets you swiftly deal with any sudden creepers or hostile mobs you might not have been prepared to take on.
/give	Get your hands on any item with this command. Simply type the desired item, target and quantity (ex. /give <player> apple 99) and voila.
/day	Sick of the night terrors? Dodge it all together - use this command to set the time of your world (ex. /time set day)

Commands are exclusive to desktop editions of Minecraft. To use a command, simply type / to open up the console, and then enter the command text.

MINECRAFT IRL

Minecraft has gotten so huge that it's become impossible to contain it within its own virtual walls. The game has both welcomed real world guests into its realm and also been welcomed by real world guests out in, well, the real world. How many of these collaborations did you catch IRL?

ANGRY BIRDS X MINECRAFT

Classic mobile game Angry Birds collaborated with Minecraft to bring a Minecraft DLC that lets players fling birds at insolent pigs. Basically, it lets players play Angry Birds with a Minecraft style. This mash-up brings the best of two iconic games together.

PRINGLES
X MINECRAFT

Did anyone see this collaboration coming? Pringles released a limited edition flavour of their crisps dedicated to Minecraft: suspicious spew. Um… thanks, Pringles? Okay, the actual flavour profile was significantly better than what you're likely imagining; more smokey and spicy than suspicious.

BAPE
X MINECRAFT

The collaboration between streetwear brand BAPE and Minecraft brought the game to real world clothing designs. A limited edition collection of oversized hoodies and sweatshirts sported the brand's trademark camo and the creeper's frozen expression of endless horror.

LACOSTE
X MINECRAFT

Welcome to Croco Island! This DLC package with Lacoste included a tennis court, mini-game and, of course, Lacoste-themed skins (thirty, if you're curious). This collaboration went both ways, with Minecraft also making an appearance in a limited edition Lacoste collection in March.

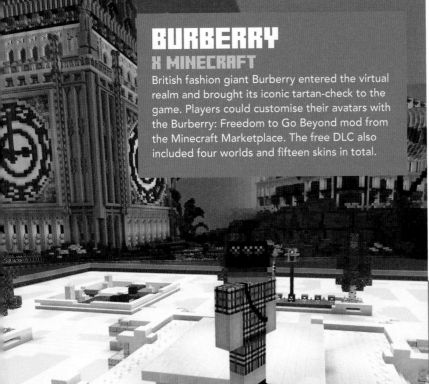

BURBERRY
X MINECRAFT

British fashion giant Burberry entered the virtual realm and brought its iconic tartan-check to the game. Players could customise their avatars with the Burberry: Freedom to Go Beyond mod from the Minecraft Marketplace. The free DLC also included four worlds and fifteen skins in total.

DUNGEONS & DRAGONS
X MINECRAFT

Dungeons & Dragons is one of the OG fantasy games. The collaboration between D&D and Minecraft allows players to deliver the classic campaigns that D&D is known for within the world of Minecraft. The DLC lets players play as their favourite character class in locations like Icewind Dale and Candlekeep to take on some of the tabletop game's classic beasties - even the big bad, the mindflayer

LEGO
X MINECRAFT

A match made in block heaven, Lego and Minecraft just makes too much sense. Lego's Minecraft sets allow players to build their own Minecraft mainstays in real life, like the Fox Lodge and the Pig House.

GUESS THE MOB

How well do you know the mobs of Minecraft? Guess the mobs below - the first hint is a question, and the second hint is the scrambled name. Can you get them all? Check out p. 62-63 for answers.

1 You don't want to come across me in the dark.
A D W R N E

2 Keep me around to keep your home safe.
T O O E C L

3 I keep an eye on the villages..
N R G M L O O E I

4 I'll help you light up those shipwrecks.
W Q U D L G O S I

5 I'm not the best catch to eat.
F F H S F U P I R E

6 Find me in the lush caves biome.
X O A L L T O

7 I love to eat magma cubes and slimes.
G F O R

8 My favourite place to perch is your shoulder.
T P R A R O

9 I'm a rare find that only hatches from an egg.
F E S N I F R

10 Look me in the eye and it's time to fight.
A R E M E D N N

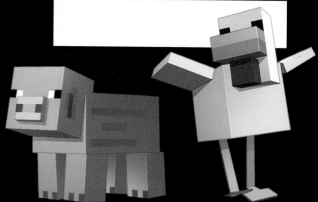

DESIGN YOUR OWN SKIN

Steve, Alex and co. may be cool, but sometimes it's more fun to raid villages as a space ninja, or take on the ender dragon as Minnie Mouse (hey, whatever floats your boat). What's your dream Minecraft skin?

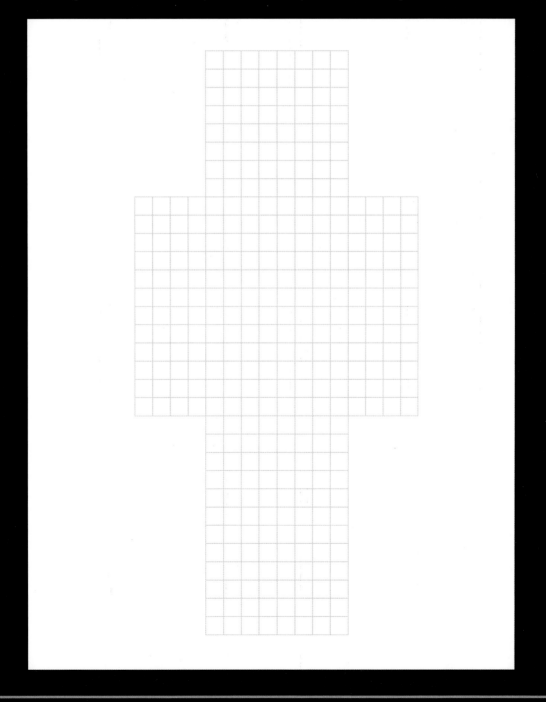

SPOT THE DIFFERENCE

Can you spot the six differences between these two images? Check out p. 62-63 for answers.

MINECRAFT CROSSWORD

Can you solve the clues to fill out this Minecraft crossword? Check out the answers on p. 62-63.

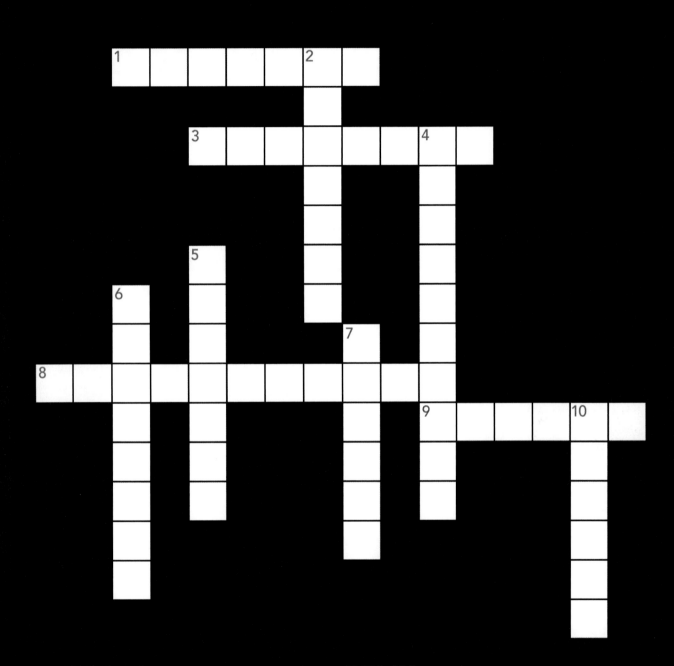

ACROSS

1. This mob can only be spawned from an egg. (7)
3. Inhabitants of the End. (8)
8. A beautiful pink biome. (6, 5)
9. A red and hellish dimension. (6)

DOWN

2. A favourite of trading villagers. (7)
4. A great enchantment for tools. (10)
5. The foundation of the Minecraft world. (7)
6. This process requires a furnace. (8)
7. The wonderful developers of Minecraft. (6)
10. Fly high! Well, glide, anyway. (6)

MINECRAFT STREAMERS

Given that it's officially the biggest-selling video game of all time, it should come as no surprise that the game has a huge presence in the streaming world. Regardless of the time of year, or even day, you'll be able to find Minecraft in the top titles being streamed on Twitch or YouTube Gaming.

So who's worth watching? Here's our list of the best of the best Minecraft streamers.

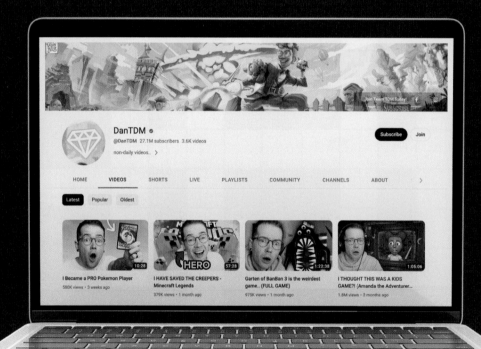

DANTDM

There's no other option to start off a Minecraft streamer recommendation list than DanTDM. As the most subscribed Minecraft YouTuber (and one of the biggest channels on the platform), DanTDM has been going strong since July 2012, amassing over 27 million subscribers and almost 20 billion channel views (just for perspective: the earth's population is around 8 billion. Let that sink in for a second). Dan even made it into the official world lore, with

an appearance in *A Portal to Mystery* (episode 6) in *Minecraft: Story Mode*!
Where to Watch:
• **YouTube** • **Twitch**

> Best Known For:
> Unbeatable subscriber
> and view counts

ETHOSLAB

Best known for his long running single-player Minecraft LP series, Ethos has been a big figure in the Minecraft streaming scene since the series started back in 2010. He plays both vanilla and modded versions of the game. He even had a joke block dedicated to him in Minecraft's April Fools Update - the Etho Slab (get it?).

Where to Watch:
• **YouTube**

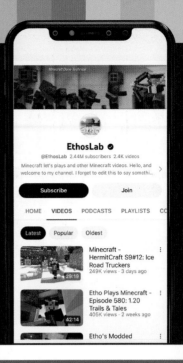

Best Known For:
A long-standing single player series

PIXLRIFFS

Pixlriffs is a great source for any Minecraft player looking to hone their skills by watching fun and accessible tutorials. Other than his popular Minecraft Survival Guide, he also provides guides on all sorts of specific gameplay scenarios, like *How to Cure Zombie Villagers*, *Setting Up Your Storage Room* and *Finding the Perfect World Seed*.

Where to Watch:
• **YouTube** • **Twitch**

Best Known For:
Great tutorials both general and in-depth.

STAMPY

Stampy (or Stampylonghead, if you're feeling formal) is a very famous name in the Minecraft scene. He is best known for his storytelling series through the voice of the Stampy Cat. He is a huge pioneer in the Minecraft edutainment sphere, with his series Wonder Quest just one of his impressive Minecraft accolades. Like DanTDM, he also made an appearance in *A Portal to Mystery* (episode 6) in *Minecraft: Story Mode*.

Where to Watch:
• **YouTube**

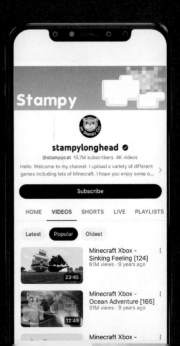

Best Known For:
Storytelling and edutainment.

PUZZLE ANSWERS

28-29 WHERE ARE STEVE AND ALEX?

37 MASTER YOUR CRAFT

1. Compass
2. Glass
3. Torch
4. Campfire
5. Loom
6. Ladder
7. Honey Block
8. Map
9. Furnace

38 SPOT THE DIFFERENCE

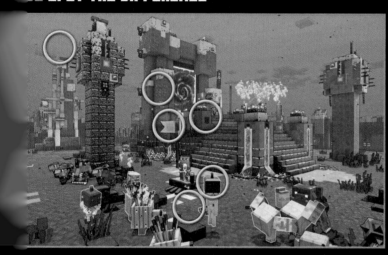

39 MINERAL MIX-UP

1. Iron
2. Diamond
3. Gold
4. Amethyst
5. Emerald
6. Lapis Lazuli
7. Obsidian
8. Coal
9. Copper

46 WORDSEARCH